# YouTube
## GROWTH HACKS

# YouTube
## GROWTH HACKS

### GAIN FIRST
### 1000 FOLLOWERS FAST

## WIJE DISSANAYAKE

MPhil (Mass Communication), MSc (Digital Marketing/ UK),
BA (Mass Media), Dip (IT), Dip (Dev Journalism),
Dip (Digital Marketing)

Disclaimer: The information contained in this book is for general informational purposes only. The author and publisher are not responsible for the outcomes of applying the techniques and knowledge in this book. The information is provided on an "as is" basis without warranties.

ISBN: 9798867126063
Published by Wije Dissanayake
Cover Design: Author
Interior Design: Author

For permission requests, please reach out to the publisher at dissaa@gmail.com.

Library of Congress Cataloging-in-Publication Data
Dissanayake, Wije.
YouTube Growth Hacks / Wije Dissanayake.
ISBN: 9798867126063

To all the aspiring content creators who want to take their YouTube journey to new heights.

*For*

*Ben*

*&*

*Shen*

# Contents

## 6. Monetization and Revenue

- Understanding AdSense
- Exploring Affiliate Marketing
- Merchandise and Sponsorships

## 7. Community Building

- Responding to Comments
- Hosting Live Streams
- Running Contests and Giveaways

## 8. Avoiding Common Pitfalls

- Copyright Issues
- Burnout and Stagnation
- Dealing with Haters

## 9. Conclusion

- Celebrating Milestones
- Continuing Your YouTube Journey

# Introduction

With over two billion monthly logged-in users worldwide, YouTube has become a popular and influential platform for content creators to share their interests, ideas, and skills. It's an exciting time to be a part of the YouTube community, with creators from all walks of life showcasing their creativity and talent. If you're reading this book, you're likely interested in becoming a successful YouTuber yourself.

The journey to success on YouTube is a challenging one. While the platform offers a vast audience, the competition is fierce, and the algorithm can be challenging to navigate. However, you can gain a following quickly and effectively with the right strategies, tips, and tricks. This book is designed to guide you through every step of your YouTube journey, from finding your niche to creating compelling content, understanding the nuances of YouTube's algorithm, promoting your channel, interacting with your audience, and monetizing your passion.

Reaching 1000 followers on YouTube is an important milestone, as it opens the door to many valuable features, such as monetization, live streaming, and community engagement. It signifies your channel's potential for growth and success. However, it takes effort and dedication to achieve this goal. This book provides essential strategies to help you reach your 1000-follower goal and set the foundation for continued growth beyond that.

Whether you're a beginner or have already gained traction on YouTube, you'll find valuable insights to supercharge your efforts in this book. By the end of this book, you'll have the knowledge and confidence to propel your channel forward and turn your YouTube dreams into reality.

So, let's embark on this exciting journey together and dive into the world of YouTube growth hacks. Let's take your channel to the next level!

# Chapter 1

# Finding Your Niche

Choosing a niche is one of the most critical decisions for a YouTuber. Your niche is your content's focus, and it defines what your channel is all about. It's the foundation upon which your YouTube journey is built, and getting it right is essential for attracting and retaining your target audience.

In this chapter, we'll explore the steps to find your niche, understand why it's crucial, and how it plays a pivotal role in achieving your goal of gaining 1000 followers in record time.

## 2.1 Identifying Your Passion

Consider your passions and interests before diving into the mechanics of choosing a niche. What do you love doing in your spare time? What topics or activities genuinely excite you? Your passion will be the fuel that keeps your channel running, especially in the early stages when you need to see significant growth.

## 2.2 Researching Popular Niches

While your passion is essential, evaluating the popularity and competition within potential niches is crucial. Some niches have more room for growth than others. Look at trends and see if your passion aligns with these areas. Consider the following:

- Trend analysis tools: Platforms like Google Trends and YouTube Trends can provide insights into popular topics and seasonal trends.
- Keyword research: Tools like Google Keyword Planner or YouTube's built-in search bar can help you identify search terms related to your interests. You can also use third-party keyword research tools.
- Competition analysis: Study successful channels within potential niches. What are they doing right? What gaps can you fill?

## 2.3 The Value of Uniqueness

Your niche doesn't have to be unique but should reflect your perspective and approach. What makes you different from others creating similar content? Whether it's your personality, style, or a unique twist on the niche, showcasing your distinctiveness will help you stand out and attract a dedicated audience.

Remember, your niche isn't set in stone. As you gain experience and grow on YouTube, you can evolve your content and shift your place if needed. However, changes should align with your core interests and audience feedback.

Your niche is the cornerstone of your YouTube journey. It's the starting point for creating content that resonates with your viewers. Finding the right balance between your passion, market demand, and unique perspective will lead you to success. In the following chapters, we'll explore leveraging your niche to create engaging content that captivates your audience and brings you one step closer to your 1000 followers goal.

# Chapter 2

# Content Creation

One of the most fundamental pillars of your YouTube channel's success is the quality of your content. In this chapter, we'll delve into the critical strategies for creating engaging and compelling content that will attract viewers and keep them returning for more.

## Quality vs. Quantity

It's a common misconception that churning out many videos guarantees rapid growth. While consistency is essential (which we'll discuss in later chapters), the quality of your content should always be a top priority.

## Tips for Ensuring Quality Content:

- **Plan Your Content:** Before hitting the record button, plan your content meticulously. Decide on the topic, structure, and key points you want to cover. Having a well-thought-out script or outline can make a significant difference.

- **Invest in Equipment:** While you don't need expensive equipment to start, investing in a decent camera, microphone, and lighting setup can significantly improve the quality of your videos.

- **Editing Matters:** Spend time editing your videos to remove mistakes, add engaging transitions, and enhance the viewing experience. Free and paid video editing software options cater to all skill levels.

- **Audio Quality:** Bad audio can drive viewers away faster than poor video quality. Ensure clear and crisp sound by using a good microphone and reducing background noise.

- Engaging Thumbnails: Create eye-catching thumbnails that accurately represent your content. A compelling thumbnail can be the difference between someone clicking on your video or scrolling past it.

## Crafting Engaging Thumbnails

Thumbnails are the gateway to your content, often determining whether a viewer clicks on your video. Here's how to create attention-grabbing thumbnails:

- **High-Quality Images:** Use high-resolution images relevant to your video's topic.

- **Contrasting Colors:** Use contrasting colours to make your text and images stand out. This will make your thumbnails more visually appealing.

- **Text Overlay:** Add a concise and engaging title or a few keywords on the thumbnail to give potential viewers an idea of your video.

- **Consistency:** Maintain a consistent style for your thumbnails to create a recognizable brand image for your channel.

## Video Editing Tips

Video editing is a skill worth mastering, which can significantly enhance the viewing experience. Here are some editing tips:

- **Trimming and Cutting:** Remove unnecessary parts, long pauses, or mistakes to keep your video concise and engaging.

- **Transitions:** Use smooth transitions between clips to avoid abrupt changes and maintain viewer interest.

- **Text and Graphics:** Add text overlays, graphics, or animations to highlight key points or provide additional context.

- **Background Music:** Background music can set the tone for your video and keep viewers engaged. However, be cautious not to overpower your voice or distract from your content.

## Utilizing Keywords

It is essential to use relevant keywords to improve the visibility of your video. Please ensure that you include appropriate keywords for better search results. Make sure to use relevant and specific keywords to enhance the discoverability of your video. The YouTube search algorithm relies on keywords to understand and suggest your content to users. Here's how to make the most of keywords:

- **Keyword Research:** Use keyword research tools to find relevant and popular search terms for your video's topic.

- **Include Keywords in Titles and Descriptions:** Incorporate these keywords into your video title, description, and tags. This helps the algorithm understand what your video is about.

- **Natural Integration:** Ensure that keywords are naturally integrated into your content. Avoid keyword stuffing, as it can negatively affect your video's ranking.

In this chapter, we've explored the foundations of content creation on YouTube. Remember that while quality is paramount, consistency and understanding your audience are equally important. By following these guidelines, you'll be well on your way to creating content that attracts and retains viewers on your journey to 1000 followers.

# Chapter 3

## Consistency is Key

To quickly gain 1000 followers on YouTube, consistency is critical. This includes consistently uploading videos, engaging with viewers, and promoting your channel. In this chapter, we'll discuss the importance of maintaining a regular posting schedule, staying on theme, and engaging with your audience to keep them returning for more.

### Creating a Content Schedule

Consistency starts with a well-planned content schedule. Your viewers should know when to expect new content from your channel. Here's how to create an effective content schedule:

- **Choose Posting Days:** Select specific days of the week when you'll release new videos. Stick to a schedule that suits your availability and is realistic for you to maintain.

- **Plan:** Plan your content so you have a backlog of videos. This ensures you can keep your schedule even when unexpected events arise.

- **Stick to Your Schedule:** Consistency is not just about starting but also about keeping your schedule. Regular uploads build anticipation and trust with your audience.

### Staying on Theme

Consistency extends to the themes and topics you cover on your channel. Your subscribers are interested in your content for a reason. Here's how to stay on theme effectively:

- **Identify Your Niche:** Define your niche and focus on creating content within that area of interest. This helps attract a specific audience who share your passion.

- **Plan Content Series:** Organize your content into series or playlists, making it easier for viewers to find related videos and binge-watch your content.

- **Avoid Drastic Shifts:** While it's okay to experiment with new topics occasionally, avoid sudden, drastic shifts in your content. Gradual expansions into related subjects can be more acceptable to your existing audience.

## Interacting with Your Audience

Building a community around your channel is crucial for retaining viewers and increasing your follower count. Here's how to engage with your audience effectively:

- **Respond to Comments:** Always respond to comments on your videos. Acknowledge feedback, answer questions, and engage in conversations with your viewers.

- **Hold Q&A Sessions:** Periodically host Q&A sessions where you answer questions from your audience. This personalizes your relationship with your viewers.

- **Live Streams and Premieres:** Host live streams and premieres to interact with your audience in real time. It's an excellent way to build a stronger connection and generate excitement around your content.

- **Community Posts:** Use YouTube's community tab to share updates, polls, and behind-the-scenes content with your audience. This keeps them engaged and informed.

- **Encourage User-Generated Content:** Encourage your viewers to create content related to your channel. This can include fan art, reviews, or challenges inspired by your videos.

- **Feedback and Suggestions:** Actively seek feedback and suggestions from your audience. This helps you improve your content and makes your viewers feel valued.

## Celebrating Milestones

As you progress to 1000 followers, remember to celebrate the small victories. Recognize your achievements, whether reaching 100 subscribers, receiving a certain number of views, or mastering a new video editing technique. Celebrating these milestones can motivate you and further engage your audience.

In this chapter, we've explored the significance of consistency in your YouTube journey. By creating a content schedule, sticking to your niche, and actively engaging with your audience, you'll achieve your 1000-follower goal. Remember, consistency keeps your existing followers engaged and attracts new ones who appreciate your dedication to providing valuable content.

# Chapter 4

# Promoting Your Channel

Creating great content is just the first step in growing your YouTube channel. You'll need to actively promote your channel and its content to reach your goal of gaining 1000 followers quickly. This chapter will explore strategies for effectively promoting your YouTube channel.

## Social Media Integration

Leveraging social media platforms is an excellent way to increase the visibility of your YouTube channel. Here's how to integrate social media into your YouTube promotion strategy:

- **Create Social Media Profiles:** Establish active accounts on popular social media platforms like Facebook, Twitter, Instagram, and TikTok. Use your channel name or a variation to maintain consistency.

- **Share Teasers and Updates:** Regularly post teasers, updates, and behind-the-scenes content about your YouTube videos on your social media accounts. This piques your interest and encourages your social media followers to check out your YouTube channel.

- **You can engage with Your Audience:** Interact with your followers on social media by responding to comments, starting conversations, and hosting Q&A sessions. Building a community on these platforms can drive more viewers to your YouTube videos.

- **Use Hashtags:** Include relevant hashtags in your social media posts to increase your content's discoverability. You can research popular hashtags in your niche to reach a broader audience.

## Collaborations with Other YouTubers

Collaborations with other YouTubers can significantly boost your channel's visibility and attract their followers to your content. Here's how to approach associations effectively:

- **Identify Potential Collaborators:** Look for YouTubers in your niche or related niches with a similar follower count or slightly higher. Approach them with a collaboration proposal that benefits both parties.

- **Plan Collaborative Content:** Discuss and plan the content you'll create together. It could be a joint video, a series, or any creative project that resonates with both audiences.

- **Promote Each Other:** Promote collaborative content on your channels and social media platforms. Encourage your viewers to check out your collaborator's channel and vice versa.

- **Cross-Promotion:** Cross-promote your collaborator's channel by including links or shout-outs in your videos or video descriptions.

## Utilizing YouTube Features

YouTube provides several features and tools that can help promote your channel:

- **YouTube Shorts:** Create short, engaging videos specifically for YouTube Shorts. These videos have the potential to go viral and attract new subscribers to your primary channel.

- **Playlists:** Encourage viewers to watch multiple videos by organizing them into playlists. Make sure to include descriptive titles and attractive thumbnails for your playlists.

- **End Screens and Cards:** Encourage viewers to explore more of your content by using end screens and cards to promote other videos or playlists from your channel.

- **Community Posts:** Utilize YouTube's community tab to share updates, polls, and behind-the-scenes content with your audience. Engaging with your subscribers keeps them interested and invested in your channel.

- **YouTube Premieres:** Announce your upcoming videos with a premiere, which allows viewers to chat and interact before the video goes live. This builds anticipation and engagement.

Remember that promoting your channel is an ongoing process. Regularly assess and adjust your promotion strategies based on their effectiveness. Promoting your content through social media, collaborations, and YouTube's features will quickly increase your chances of gaining 1000 followers.

# Chapter 5

## Analyzing Your Progress

Gaining 1000 followers on YouTube in record time requires more than creating and promoting content. It also involves understanding your channel's performance and making informed decisions to drive growth. This chapter will explore the importance of analyzing your progress and using data to refine your strategy.

### Using YouTube Analytics

YouTube provides a powerful analytics tool that offers insights into your channel's performance. Regularly reviewing these analytics is crucial to understanding what's working and what needs improvement. Here's how to use YouTube Analytics effectively:

- **Audience Demographics:** Understand who your viewers are, including their age, gender, location, and device preference. This information can help tailor your content to your audience's preferences.

- **Watch Time:** Pay attention to your videos' watch time. Videos with higher watch time tend to rank better and are more likely to be suggested by YouTube's algorithm.

- **Traffic Sources:** Analyze where your viewers are coming from, whether it's a YouTube search, suggested videos, or external websites. Identifying the sources of traffic that generate the most views is made easier with this feature.

- **Engagement Metrics:** Review metrics like likes, dislikes, comments, and shares. High engagement indicates that your content resonates with your audience.

- **Retention Rate:** Assess the average percentage of a video that viewers watch. Videos with higher retention rates tend to perform better in search and recommendations.

- **Click-Through Rate (CTR):** CTR measures how often viewers click on your video's thumbnail when shown to them. An attractive thumbnail and title combination can significantly boost CTR.

## Adjusting Your Strategy

Based on the insights gained from YouTube Analytics, adapting and improving your strategy is crucial. Here's how to make data-driven decisions:

- **Identify Top-Performing Content:** Discover which videos have the highest engagement, retention, and view counts. Try replicating the elements that make these videos successful in your future content.

- **Keyword Optimization:** Analyze which keywords and phrases drive traffic to your channel. Use this information to refine your content and target specific keywords more effectively.

- **A/B Testing:** Experiment with different video titles, thumbnails, and lengths to see what resonates best with your audience. Test one variable at a time to determine what makes a significant impact.

- **Content Calendar Adjustments:** Based on your audience's preferences and the types of content that perform well, adjust your content calendar. Focus on creating more of what works.

- **Engagement Strategies:** If you notice a drop in engagement, consider new ways to engage your audience, such as interactive features, contests, or live streams.

- **Collaborations and Trends:** Stay aware of current trends in your niche and consider collaborating with other creators who align with those trends.

- **Consistency and Upload Schedule:** Ensure that you're adhering to your content schedule and, if necessary, adjust the posting frequency based on your audience's response.

## Tracking Your Progress

Set specific, measurable goals and regularly track your progress toward reaching your 1000-follower milestone. This helpful tip can make staying motivated and focused on your objectives easier.

Remember that gaining followers on YouTube is a dynamic process that may require continuous adaptation. Regularly analyze your channel's performance, adjust your strategy, and learn from your successes and failures. Using data to inform your decisions, you can maximize your chances of reaching your 1000-follower goal in record time.

# Chapter 6

## Monetization and Revenue

Monetizing your YouTube channel is an exciting step to gaining 1000 followers and beyond. This chapter will explore monetization methods and strategies to generate revenue from your YouTube content.

### Understanding AdSense

Google AdSense is one of the most common ways to monetize your YouTube channel. It allows you to earn money by displaying ads on your videos. Here's how to get started with AdSense:

- **Eligibility:** To qualify for AdSense, your channel must have at least 1000 subscribers and 4000 watch hours in the past 12 months.

- **Ad Formats:** There are different ad formats, including skippable video ads, non-skippable video ads, and display ads. Experiment with these formats to find what works best for your audience.

- **Ad Placement:** Consider ad placement within your videos. You can place ads at your content's beginning, middle, or end. Balancing ad placement with viewer experience is essential.

- **Ad Revenue:** Your earnings from AdSense depend on the niche, viewer demographics, and the number of clicks and views. CPM (Cost Per Mille) is a metric that measures your earnings per 1000 views.

## Exploring Affiliate Marketing

Affiliate marketing is another way to generate revenue through your YouTube channel. Promote products or services with your unique affiliate links and earn a commission on sales. Here's how to utilize affiliate marketing effectively:

- **Choose Relevant Products or Services:** Promote products or services relevant to your channel's niche and audience. Ensure they align with your content.

- **Disclose Affiliate Links:** Be transparent with your audience by disclosing that you may earn a commission if they purchase using your affiliate links. Honesty builds trust.

- **Review and Recommend:** Provide honest and valuable reviews or recommendations for the products or services you're promoting. Explain how they can benefit your viewers.

- **Track Performance:** Monitor the performance of your affiliate links to understand which products or services resonate most with your audience. Focus on promoting what works.

## Merchandise and Sponsorships

Merchandise and sponsorships are additional monetization options that can boost your revenue. Here's how to explore these opportunities:

- **Merchandise Sales:** Design and sell branded merchandise related to your channel. This can include T-shirts, mugs, posters, or any products your audience may be interested in.

- **Sponsorships:** Collaborate with brands and companies that align with your channel's niche. Sponsored videos or product placements can generate income while providing value to your audience.

- **Maintain Authenticity:** Whether selling merchandise or partnering with sponsors, maintaining authenticity is crucial. To keep your credibility, only to endorse products or services you genuinely believe in is essential. You can just avoid promoting anything that you do not have faith in.

### Diversify Your Income Streams

To maximize your revenue potential, consider diversifying your income streams. Limiting your income to a single method can restrict your earnings. You can create a more stable income by combining AdSense, affiliate marketing, merchandise sales, and sponsorships.

## Compliance and Legal Considerations

When monetizing your channel, you must comply with YouTube's policies and relevant laws, including copyright and disclosure regulations. Familiarize yourself with the rules and ensure you're adhering to them.

### Building a Long-Term Strategy

Monetization is a complex fix for instant income. It requires a long-term strategy and consistent effort. Remember that while revenue is essential, it should not compromise the quality and integrity of your content.

As you continue your journey to gain 1000 followers and beyond, monetization can provide a source of income that allows you to reinvest in your channel and improve your content. You can create a sustainable revenue stream from your YouTube channel by understanding and effectively utilizing AdSense, affiliate marketing, merchandise, sponsorships, and adhering to legal requirements.

# Chapter 7

# Community Building

Building a solid and engaged community around your YouTube channel is essential for your channel's growth and for creating a supportive and interactive environment for your viewers. This chapter will explore strategies for fostering a thriving community to help you reach your 1000-follower goal.

## Responding to Comments

One of the most straightforward ways to build a community is by actively engaging with your audience. Responding to comments on your videos is a powerful way to connect with your viewers. Here's how to do it effectively:

- **Timely Responses:** Try responding to comments as soon as possible, shortly after you publish a video. This shows that you value your viewers' input.

- **Encourage Conversations:** Ask questions or seek opinions within your videos to encourage viewers to leave comments. The more engagement, the more your video is promoted by YouTube.

- **Positive and Constructive Feedback:** Respond to both positive and negative comments respectfully and constructively. This fosters a positive and inclusive community.

## Hosting Live Streams

Live streaming is an excellent way to interact with your audience in real time. You can answer questions, share updates, and play games or create content together. Here's how to make the most of live streams:

- **Schedule Regular Live Streams:** Announce your live streams in advance and stick to a schedule. This helps your audience know when to expect your live interactions.

- **Engage in Real-Time:** Interact with your viewers, read and respond to their comments, and address their questions or concerns.

- **Plan Interactive Activities:** You should consider hosting Q&A sessions, challenges, or live collaborations with other creators to keep your audience engaged and entertained.

## Running Contests and Giveaways

Contests and giveaways can generate excitement and encourage viewers to participate actively in your channel's community. If you are looking to run successful contests and giveaways, here are some valuable tips that you should keep in mind:

- **Clear Rules and Prizes:** Ensure the rules and prizes are well-defined and transparent. Make sure your viewers understand how to participate and what they can win.

- **Promote Actively:** Use various platforms, including your YouTube channel, social media, and email newsletters, to promote your contest or giveaway.

- **Encourage User-Generated Content:** You should consider contests that require your viewers to create content related to your channel, such as fan art, reviews, or challenges inspired by your videos.

- **Celebrate Winners:** Announce the winners in an exciting and celebratory way. This builds anticipation for future contests and acknowledges your community's involvement.

## Building a Community Tab

YouTube offers a "Community" tab for channels with over 1000 subscribers. Use this feature to share updates, polls, and behind-the-scenes content with your audience. It's an excellent way to keep your subscribers engaged and informed.

## Moderation and Healthy Discussions

As your community grows, consider appointing moderators to help maintain a healthy and respectful environment. Encourage open discussions, but set clear guidelines for respectful communication. Remove or report inappropriate or offensive comments when necessary to uphold the quality of your community.

## Consistency in Community Building

Consistency is not limited to content creation; it also extends to community building. Engaging with your audience, hosting live streams, and running contests should be regular and reliable aspects of your channel's activities.

Remember that your community is the backbone of your YouTube channel's success. By responding to comments, hosting live streams, running contests and giveaways, and actively participating in your community's discussions, you can create a thriving, supportive, and engaged following that will contribute to your journey to 1000 followers and beyond.

# Chapter 8

# Avoiding Common Pitfalls

As you work towards gaining 1000 followers on YouTube, you must be aware of common pitfalls that can hinder your progress and potentially damage your channel's growth. This chapter will explore these challenges and provide strategies to navigate them effectively.

## Copyright Issues

Copyright infringement is a significant concern for YouTubers. Using copyrighted material without permission can result in demonetization, video removal, or channel strikes. Learn how to avoid copyright issues:

- **Use Royalty-Free Music and Media:** When incorporating music, images, or videos into your content, use royalty-free or licensed materials to ensure you have the right to use them.

- **Attribute Properly:** If you use content under a Creative Commons license, provide proper attribution as required by the permit.

- **Fair Use:** Understand the "fair use" concept for copyrighted material. It may allow you to use limited portions of copyrighted content for commentary, criticism, news reporting, or educational purposes, but the rules can vary by region and specific cases.

- **Seek Permission:** If you need clarification on using a particular content, please ask the copyright holder or use licensed content.

## Burnout and Stagnation

Creating and maintaining a YouTube channel can be demanding, and it's not uncommon for creators to experience burnout or stagnation. Here's how to avoid these pitfalls:

- **Set Realistic Goals:** Ensure your content schedule and goals are realistic and sustainable. Overextending yourself can lead to burnout.

- **Take Breaks:** Regularly take breaks to recharge and prevent burnout. Plan time for relaxation and creative rejuvenation.

- **Experiment and Evolve:** To combat stagnation, experiment with new content ideas, formats, and styles. Keep your channel fresh and exciting for your audience.

- **Engage with Your Audience:** Staying connected with your viewers through comments, live streams, and community posts can rejuvenate your channel and provide fresh content ideas.

## Dealing with Haters

Criticism and negative comments are an unfortunate part of being on YouTube. It's essential to handle hate comments and negativity with grace and professionalism:

- **Stay Professional:** Respond to hate comments professionally and respectfully, or consider ignoring them. Engaging respectfully can diffuse a difficult situation.

- **Use Moderation Tools:** Use YouTube's moderation tools to hide, remove, or report inappropriate comments or users. Create a positive and respectful atmosphere on your channel.

- **Focus on Positivity:** Emphasize the importance of positive and constructive feedback on your track. Encourage discussions that are beneficial for both you and your audience.

- **Develop Resilience:** Haters and negative comments are an unfortunate part of online visibility. Develop resilience and focus on the support and appreciation of your true fans.

## 9. Conclusion

As you progress toward gaining 1000 followers on YouTube and beyond, you must remain aware of the common pitfalls that can affect your channel's growth and well-being. By avoiding copyright issues, managing burnout, and handling negativity professionally, you can navigate these challenges effectively and continue on your path to YouTube success. Stay committed, keep learning, and remember that every challenge is an opportunity for growth.

*- End -*